AF615016

MYSTIC MOMENTS

Frances Grant Nachant

Mystic Moments

To dear Elizabeth
with love

Frances Grant Nachant

THE GOLDEN QUILL PRESS
Publishers
Francestown New Hampshire

Library of Congress Catalog Card Number 78-51853

ISBN 0-8233-0275-X

Printed in the United States of America

Dedicated to God
Father Creator
of my soul
and
Giver of all Good
And Perfect Gifts

ACKNOWLEDGEMENTS AND THANKS

My sincere thanks to the editors of the following publications in which many of my poems appeared: *Cyclotron; The Archer; United Poets; Message; American Bard; Sharing Magazine of Christian Healing; The Saint-New York; Ideals; Flamingo; Cyclo-Flame; Prairie Poets; American Poets; Poet-India; The Showcase; Swordsman Review; National Catholic Press Syndicate; Let's Have a Chat,* Tokyo, Japan; *One Hundred Years of Alaskan Poetry; Orphic Lute; Haiku-Highlights; Nine Muses* Vol. 1 & 2; *International Hall of Fame Poets,* Vol. 1 & 2; *Etta Murphy Awards Books,* Vol. 1 & 2; *Alaska Star Weekly; Wagging Tales; Spring Anthology,* Mitre Press, London; *Academia Leonardo Da Vinci,* Rome; *Windless Orchard,* Indiana University Press; *Golden Quill Anthology* 1970 & 1971; *Christmas Portraits; Haiku and Tanka Anthology; International Who's Who in Poetry Anthology* Vol. 1, London; *Selected Poems* Vol. 1967, 1968, & 1969; *Masters of Modern Poetry,* Rome; *International Poetry Review; Poetry Forum,* Kansas; *Hyacinths and Biscuits; Laurel Leaves; The Muse,* Alba De Oro, Rome; *Poetry Hour; 200th Commemorative Anthology;* Radio - Canadian National Radio Network, Sta. KBBW San Diego, California; T.V. Sta. 39 and 50.

CONTENTS

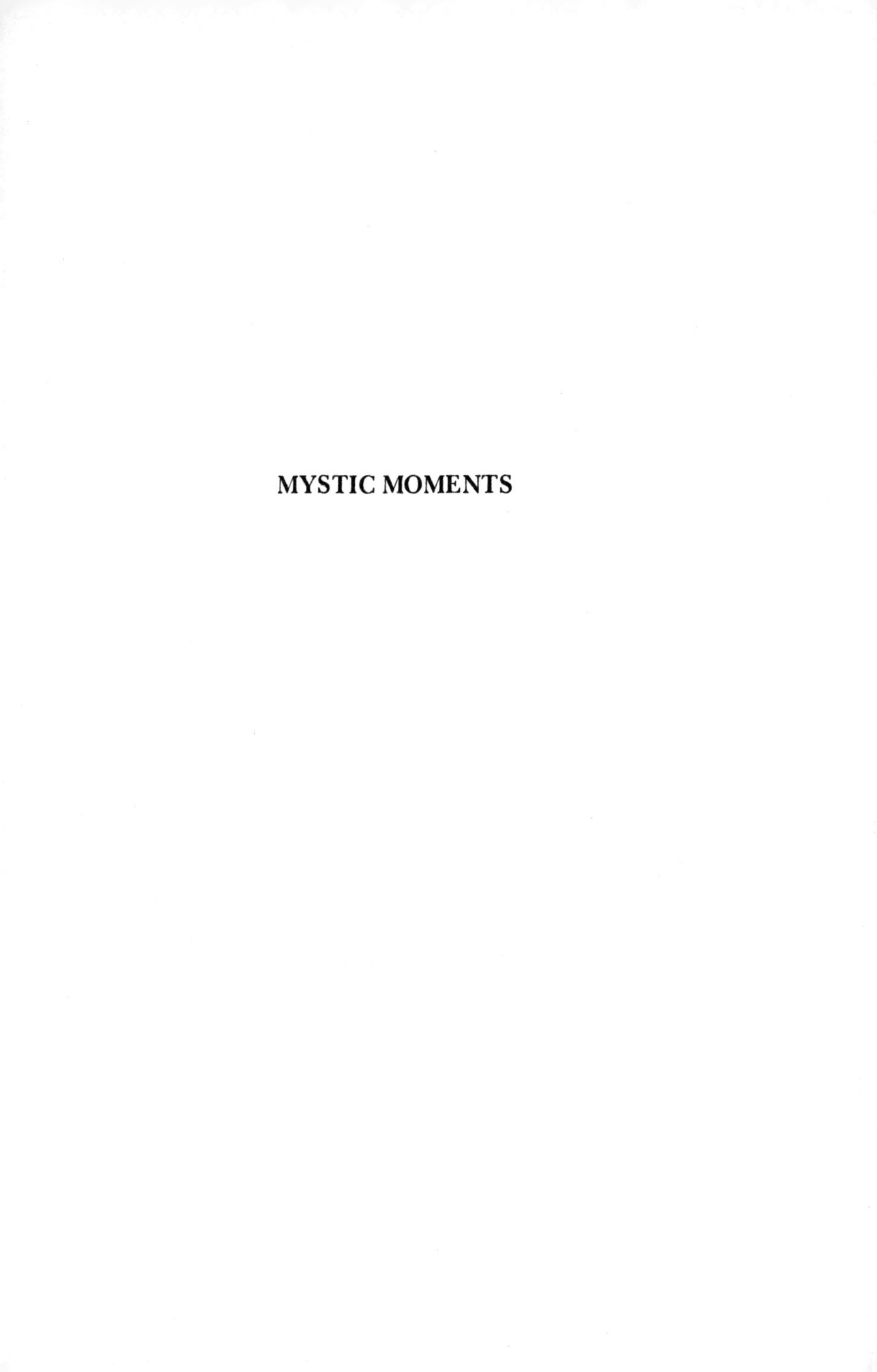

MYSTIC MOMENTS

The most beautiful and most profound emotion we can experience is the sensation of the mystical. It is the sower of all true Science. He to whom this emotion is a stranger, who can no longer stand in awe, is as good as dead. That deep emotional conviction of the presence of a superior reasoning power, which is revealed in the incomprehensible Universe, forms my idea of God. — Dr. Albert Einstein.

SIBYL PETALS

Deep in the Soul of God
My poem lies
From well-springs of the soul
My song will rise
When melody starts to roll
Effulgence will bring surprise.

SOUL CHILD

Watch him turn the leaves of the book
And then take another good look:
Angels, Prophets, demons and saints,
Truth and Love, bearing no complaints.

Flying to planets and the stars
Will explore the moon and Mars,
Satellites, comets, cosmic dust, moonbeams,
Prophecies, portraits, hopes and dreams.

We will travel in the grandest style
Bringing messages to ever beguile
With Faith's Philosophy most profound
Mysteries of eternal life will propound.

THE POET-SEER

He always sees in the fourth dimension
Despite mankind's common contention,
To spiritual realms the Seer turns his face;
God's Presence reaches into Infinite space.

To me Infinite Presence is ever nigh,
Plus unlimited horizons of earth and sky;
Being steeped in the metaphysical
We are never blind to the eternal.

Sometimes we become martyr to the cause.
When finite man with limited sight will pause,
Mired in the quicksands of the material,
He is prone to scoff at the Seer's tale.

Because spiritual values are lasting
When man ceases arguing and blasting,
He will soon find vision's reality
For prophecy is not born of phantasy.

O human soul! Shedding darkness for light
Enables you to share the Seer's sight.
In higher realms the Prophet will function,
A mission decreed by sacred unction.

THE GREATEST PROPHET

A child busy in laughing play,
Neighbor children running about,
Happy, carefree, romping alway
And with many a happy shout.

Then God spoke to the child-mystic
"Go practice on the piano. In time
You will greatly need your music
To support your future children."

Quite startling in the midst of play!
There were no questions – no retort
But only God's will to obey . . .
Later there were three to support.

Music solved the pressing problem
Obeying Him, I never forget,
Through piano lessons I fed them.
The Greatest Prophet is God as yet!

IN ST. JOHN'S CHURCH

It all happened as God willed
The child was on her knees,
When His angels appeared
and spoke to the child –
"You may come with us now.
If you remain in this world
it will mean great suffering."
"I will see it through,
to God's will I bow.
The Lord Jesus is standing by me now,"
answered the frail
twelve year old mystic.
"Christ did not complain, why should I?
God shares His love and wisdom too.
To do His will is all I ask
No matter how hard the task."

SOLILOQUY

Absolute conviction, perfect assurance
When logic and all outward insistence
Argued against the marvellous prophecy.
Was it God who spoke most tenderly?
Destiny decreed this should be it.
To hear with the blessed ears of spirit,
Through the Superconscious, seeing,
In tune with His Infinite Being.

Miraculous when God reached my mind;
His message came in perfect truth divined,
And many wondrous miracles of healing.
For these in gratitude I am kneeling;
For blessings received with humility
I owe a share to Him for this ability:
In prophecy I echo the Lord's voice
By Divine Decree, not only by choice.

17 – And it shall come to pass in the last days, saith God, I will pour out my Spirit upon all flesh; and your sons and your daughters shall prophecy, and your young men shall see visions, and your old men shall dream dreams;

18 – And on my servants and my handmaidens I will pour out in those days of my Spirit; and they shall prophecy.

19 – And I will shew wonders in heaven above, and signs in the earth beneath; blood and fire and vapor of smoke. – Acts Chapter 2, The Holy Bible.

THE MYSTERY OF PROPHECY

Sometimes it comes in dreams at night
Again it comes in broad daylight
Prophets gifted by God above
Speak prophecy from His pure love.

Prescience may come in childhood stage,
Is not bestowed by worldly sage,
Is not won in college degree,
Only from God through Eternity.

False prophets give only falsehood
Worshipping images of wood.
God works through a trustworthy mind,
In His prophet the truth you find.

From mediums, confusion often rolls,
Through the works of demon controls
Most horrible tales can be told
In the crossing of palms with gold.

Sneaking devils confuse the mind
Whispering, tempting from behind
Messages from God are not sold,
Through Prophets the Truth is foretold.

THE WHITE BIRD'S CRY

Words go rolling by
As the white bird's cry
Lend thy ear, O ear of the soul,
While passing by, each winged bird
With message carried, may be heard.
In its beak a key is held
Designed to open heaven's gate.
Now I wait, I wait, I wait . . . .
For the White bird's cry.
May the message not pass me by.

IMMORTALITY

When my son was just a year old baby
sitting on his grandmother's knee
he taught me about God and immortality.
"Out of the mouths of babes the truth shall come."
The great spiritual facts are revealed to some,
for missions of Love and Peace arise therefrom.

Looking very innocent, yet ever so wise,
cherub with softly curled hair and blue eyes,
pointing his infant hand toward the skies,
said "I went up to heaven and came back again."
Truth was revealed to me there and then!
Who taught this babe about Heaven? When?

Startled, I hardly realized the full
import of words strangely metaphysical.
Suddenly meaning, wonderfully whole,
began to dawn upon my mind. Soul-wise
the veil was lifted from my eyes.
I glimpsed a Pearl, wondrous prize.

My soul now sings of joy and praise,
tuned to celestial music of the spheres.
A light shines, knowledge, true belief;
no longer thoughts of death nor grief
for loved ones departed from our midst.
Faith, the door to Life, dispels the mist.

GOD'S DECREE?

A vision of Europe's battlefields soaked in blood
From the flower of manhood, a terrible flood.
In sorrow for every Mother's wounded son,
The heart of all motherhood with mine was one.

Christmas week – the children in chorus singing
"PEACE ON EARTH"
And there is no peace! War has not ceased.
The horrors, the violence has increased.
Then the voice of God speaking to me
In the blessed assurance of prophecy.

Telling my daughter Trudy that her brother
Will come home alive from the war;
In my prophetic powers putting great store,
She replied "You have always been right mother,
I know Grant will come back as you say,
And we will be proud of him someday."

A Vision
(Doctors bending over son's still form)

An airplane flew him to the British Isles.
He had led his men over many tedious miles,
His Captain was shot down before his eyes
A Buddy, whose life and friendship was a prize
My young Lieutenant stepped into his shoes
World War II horrors are no longer news.

The doctor said, "Medical science is finished,
Only a miracle from God can do it now."
I replied "You will see a miracle!" I made my vow,
Renewed my covenant there and then.
We have finished with the works of men.
In faith, to God in prayer I went
From His Spirit, the answer was sent.

The message which came through my soul
Was clearly, "Your son is now made whole."
Again conviction of the prophecy crystallized,
The prediction, hugged to my heart, long prized.

Now a Research Scientist, he has come through
In the pattern of his life as a child, I knew.
He belongs to the group of unsung heroes,
In science, finding answers only God knows.

EMBRYO SCIENTIST

(To My Son)

Who hears the world
turning around?
Does it squeak?
Does it creak?
Who oiled the axis
that spins underground?
Where does it begin?
Where is it found?
For eons it turns,
yet never makes a sound!

THE SHADOW

Election Day – November 1960
I am tuned in on television
How happy I am
That John F. Kennedy is winning!
For we sing the same
Song of Peace.

A dark shadow falls across his face!
Softly, mysteriously,
My spirit hears the unwritten message,
A wail comes from my soul,
Cries of apprehension in prediction,
Tears of liquid fire
Flow from my heart;
The devil's own won't let him live!
He is too great a man
He will be assassinated!
Terror of prescience weighed upon my mind
And moved my soul to prayer.
The shadow that fell across his face
Was the shape of the Cross.

From *Song of Peace* by Author

COPALIS

Copalis Beach is now a magic word
Where our Lord's voice was clearly heard
On a Pacific shore at journey's end.
Coming into view around the bend
Was a lovely strand at ocean's edge,
And above all this a forest hedge.

Seen riding the surf was a sea bird;
Roar of breakers was plainly heard
While we watched the foaming ocean waves
On a beach once trod by Indian braves.
Yet no works of man had marred the scene;
On blue waters the sun left its sheen.

Coastline miles curved blind turns of shore.
We were not satisfied, we must see more.
Back into our new car we all piled.
Eager to see, the children all smiled,
Angels, unaware of vicious quicksands;
Talking clam chowder, dug by all hands.

Awful suction of quicksand was felt
Thinking what a tragic deal fate has dealt,
Terrible fear by all of us was shown
Most awful feeling we had ever known.
Nowhere in sight were any strong men.
Thus calmly and quickly I prayed again.

My Mother's tears were almost flowing,
I spoke calmly with assurance glowing

"Keep calm Mother dear. Help is coming."
Mother listened, quieted instantly.
We faced the impending catastrophe
From the roaring waves debauchery.

Huge swells could crush and smash the car.
Wreckage pieces were strewn near and far.
Our car was threatened by rising tide!
We knew the Lord was on our side.
Although hubs were buried in quicksand
Almighty God can always take a hand.

No time to hunt human help, just pray;
Heaven took over on a summer day.
Contrary to outward insistence . . .
A miracle of Blessed Assurance!
Strong horses coming around the bend
Soon pulled the car out at journey's end.

PRESCIENCE
(1929)

I see visions of rocket ships
See tragic failure of some trips.
Man to other planets can fly!
I see what God has done on high.
Seeing reality, complete and rare,
A prophecy never decried,
By our scientists never denied.

Visioned planets, vast, clean and fair
Long before man could travel there
Worlds prepared by the Creator.
Scientists, inventors work to conquer
Space and gravity, problems of air;
Then lifting man by rocket fire
To explore the moon, in space attire.

Exploring Mars, another goal,
To find fair mansions for the soul;
Platting cities by minds quite keen
Better than any Earth has seen
With wider streets and cleaner air
No parking problems unconquered be
No slums, no plagues, germ and smog free.

No wars, nor cruel violence;
Destructive sinners outside the fence;
No huge lumbering dinosaurs
As were on this old Earth of ours,

But intelligence arriving there
With plans of organization
Hurled by rocket-fire explosion.

By telephone hearing from Moon and Mars,
Television apparatus on stars.
This vision is clearly projected
I see rocket ships perfected.
Genius reflects God's omniscience,
Progress controlled by His providence;
He gives the signal to go ahead.
This prophecy is ended, enough said.

THE LILY GIRL

While walking one Sunday afternoon,
On a bright day in the month of pleasures
Seeing some fragrant wild flowers
I stopped to gather these treasures,
While mother sat to rest on a big log.
What sweet joy grows in that mossy bog,
White lilies unadorned and unashamed,
Delicate scent no artist ever framed.

As I stooped to pick another lily
Suddenly a thought came willy-nilly
My cherished friend just passed away;
The very hour proved true and the day.
Death put out the candle of life too soon.
God's message came at two in the afternoon
Over a thousand miles of land and sea.
How marvelous is God's telepathy!

Note: My dear friend passed on at exactly 2 p.m. that Sunday afternoon.

RHYTHM OF THE UNIVERSE

God wills; here comes the dawn! The light is blessed;
Water, earth, suns, stars form at His behest.
Jehovah plans; appears the moon and tide;
Then He looks on Creation with great pride.
From His Divine Love souls of men are born;
A man and woman, smiling, greet the morn.
The Creator smiles, flowers soon appear
Expressing His great love, always so near.
He gives commandments, which comprise the Law;
Pronounced Creation good, without a flaw.
God wills; the earth, the sun orbit in space!
Then man's atomic bombs in chaos race.
Jarring rhythmic patterns of God's own world
May bring on man God's wrath in thunder hurled!

COSMIC SYMPHONY

Out-driven, lost the Eden Garden view,
Man blocked the harmonizing chords by sin,
The Song of Love drowned out in worldly din,
And pure rhythm of Heaven lost to you.
The spheric hymn of praise shut off is true;
For jarring notes of swords that clash have been,
Atomic blasts with fallout never win!
They block the blessed music's concord too.

A holy psalm now tunes my soul's refrain
Divine passion of the Christ in good-will,
The sweetest cosmic anthem heard again,
New prophecy of peace, celestial strain.
Hear joyous symphony upon the hill
As God forgives the penitential men.

Eugene Cernan, Apollo Astronaut, described the earth viewed from the moon, as "floating in an infinity of space and time. It's all too beautiful, too logical and too perfect to have happened by accident. Someone put this universe together; it was not just two dust particles that came together."

THE CROSS OF LIGHT

(December 9, 1944)

With memory's eye of photographic line
I see a glowing Cross, a flawless Sign,
Emblazoned on the dark December sky.
This phenomenon explained only by
The mystery of His unfathomed way;
The flaming Cross lights up the winter day
None but God cut into the purple pall,
Between earth and sun, it had created a wall.

What a rare and marvellous exposure!
Photographed upon my mind forever;
Phenomenal symbol of Salvation;
Divine Privileged initiation.
Diety's benign sunlight streaming through
Upon us who stood below, just we two.
No man carved this symmetrical Cross
But He whom we acknowledge Creation's Boss.

We know the Resurrection of the Lord,
The scriptures tell us of the Flaming Sword
And Burning Bush in the day of Moses;
We have all seen the Rainbow of Promise;
In December sky the Cross shone by day!
Like Star of Bethlehem pointing the way,
Its light has permeated my soul,
Proving by the Cross we are made whole.

Note: on THE CROSS OF LIGHT

My little daughter Joyce, viewing the cross in the sky and after contemplating it for several minutes, quietly remarked, "Mother, I believe it is a Sign." This was in the forenoon, December 9, 1944 at Woodinville, Washington, a very small village northeast of Seattle. It was a time when our country was involved in the most terrible war in the history of mankind.

Today as I hear over television the words of a stupid man who says "God is dead," I recall this blessed God-given sign of the cross in the sky and I know God lives! Adding to this all the Miracles we have won through prayer is blessed assurance that He lives!

TIME AND SPACE

He looked at his watch saying "I'm
Certainly running out of time,"
Then he jumped into his car
Continuing his journey far.
At eighty miles an hour he crashed
Rolled over and over and smashed;
Then he found himself out there
With nothing but time everywhere.

In the middle of Eternity
With a close up view of infinity
He gazed in search of Seraphim,
Nothing but time was left for him!
Time ahead of him, eternity all around
Looking backward, forward, to the ground,
Even to the left or to the right
Time was all there was in sight.

Suddenly he looked for God and prayed
He saw the worlds our Maker had made
Stars and planets He had hung in space
"Here the Lord of Hosts has set the pace,
All this is His manifestation,
All this is Jehovah's Creation
He is everywhere, this is His,
Where I am the Creator is."

Regardless of a sense of consternation
Suddenly came a great revelation

"Without the physical eyes, seeing!
In Him I live, move and have my being!
Infinity, eternity inseparable!
Elohim and infinity indivisible;
Time and space merged . . . Eternity!
God's magnitude is Infinity!!"

THE LONE EAGLE

In Charles Augustus Lindbergh's college days
An airplane landed near his campus site.
He quickly signed up during airplane craze
At flying school, then joined Air-Mail flight.
The wish soon grew in him to cross the sea,
To bridge the great ocean-divided lands.
Six men tried for success not meant to be,
But Lindbergh's genius met the task's demands.
When "Lone Eagle" with his silver wings turned
In non-stop flight to land at Le Bourgét,
He won the laurels he had truly earned,
The Fates by star Polaris led the way.
"Lindy" built an enduring bridge on high,
Inspired man to conquer space, to fly!

EXPLORER OF SPACE

Imagination, vision with science wed
To achieve through greatest courage and zest,
The speeding Eagle finding lunar nest;
On this the mind of today's child is fed.
We will remember those who once led,
Who rode the orbital wave at highest crest,
Dauntless courage crowned with awe impressed
By astronauts whose worthy fame will spread.
Our youngest President fostered the race
His mind reached beyond the stratosphere.
Foresight instilled the hope to land on moon;
Persuaded means to explore outer space,
Projected vision always very clear:
His faith has made this certain very soon.

Note: Written in 1963 by author. Published in author's book *Song of Peace*, 1968.

A REAL SWINGER

As a retired female Astronaut
  life could not be finer,
For America's only female Astronaut
  whose heart-beat was the center
of attention for many thousands
  on May 28, 1959.
Since her triumphant return
  she is doing fine.

Astronaut Baker blazed a 15-minute-
  1500-mile trail
through space to determine if man
  would survive or fail.
Miss Baker, a tiny Peruvian monkey
  was launched with a monkey, Able,
who survived the flight but died
  on the base operating table.

Now Miss "T.L.C." – tender loving care –
  lives in a private suite.
As a swinger she hourly performs
  a clever acrobatic feat,
barreling through her window,
  swinging on a tiny trapeze.
Our Astronaut is either eating gelatin
  or basking in shade at ease.

Swinging or munching monkey chow
  in air-conditioned temperature,

Ms. Baker, tourist attraction, is a wow
you may be sure.

Note: Miss Baker resides at Naval Aerospace
Medical Institute, Pensacola, Florida.

RENDEZVOUS IN SPACE

While planets seem motionless in space
Man's satellites are holding a race,
Are soaring at the most terrific speed
Do you wonder – why hurry? Why the need?
Men with umbilical cord fastened tight,
Are thrilled to walk in space at such height.
We will soon bridge the space between planets,
Regardless of some very unusual upsets,
Finding new frontiers to colonize by man
In this blue-print of the Creator's plan.

BEYOND THE STARS

As the satellite went into orbit
With our American Eage in it
My heart went rocketing with him,
Soaring into the stratosphere
While earthbound souls remain here;
Knowing my Prophetic vision in the past
Is being perfectly realized at last!

Each Astronaut, conqueror of space,
Rocketed beyond the eagle's flight
Is hero among heroes in our sight!
Beyond the stars he dreams of moon race,
Of photographing, televising moon's face.

LADDER TO THE STARS

Lunerauts upon the old moon
Will search and dig the virgin soil.
In weightless handicap they toil
For answers from Time's cryptic vault,
Oxygen lack is the moon's worst fault.
They hunt, spade, drill and deeply dig
Finding no bars of root or twig,
Seeking secrets of the universe.
To remain long would speed the hearse.
This stairway to the stars
Is one step closer to Mars!

MOON ENCHANTMENT

1957

We
Children
Of the sun
Must always love
Its heart-warming rays
After these dark grey days.
Poets write about the moon,
Scientists aim to get there soon.
Desolate dry deserts and craters,
Surely is not a place for you or me.

TO AN ASTRONAUT

(Gordon Cooper)

When he smiled and waved at me
I was on fifth floor balcony
Of my hotel at Waikiki
Juliet never was more thrilled,
Even the tropical birds trilled
As our space eagle's motorcade
Drove along Waikiki's esplanade.
In this close-up of our Astronaut
From a mission with danger fraught,
Impressed by his great fortitude,
New horizons have Space magnitude.

TRAGEDY OF APOLLO I

(January 1967)

Ready for the first manned rocket flight,
three astronauts talk of the thrill
of being first man in outer space;
with the eagerness of youth
fasten their space suits,
adjust accouterments,
with excitement step into the capsule
of Apollo I at Cape Kennedy.

The countdown . . . the rocket fired!
It never left the pad . . . capsule on fire.
Three astronauts martyred in the cause
of conquering space!
A nation in mourning.
Yet the Apollo Space Program will go on
changing the Dirge of Dolours
to the Song of Triumph.

BLUEPRINT OF SPACE

All my life I have gazed in wonder and awe
Upon the swinging planets that I saw
Obeying forever the higher law!

The Celestial Creation is most eloquent,
Shows relativity that is omniscient
In sun, moon, and planet Earth's alignment.

Each planet is hung in strategic place.
For eons of time this blueprint of space
Has set the stage for the human race!

By Master Mind no scientist can deny
Nor can astronomers who graph the sky.
God has written His Signature on high!

COSMOSCOPE

Seeing more and farther
   in the darkness of night
Than in the noonday hour
   of broad daylight,
Star gazing, vision reaches
   the fifth dimension,
Sunlight brilliance, an opaque
   wall of prevention,
Pulls us back to myopic
   vision of earth
From the fringe of star-rimmed
   infinite birth.

FOOTPRINTS ON THE MOON

From the galaxy of brilliant stars
Have splintered meteors left these scars?
Again with intently focused eye,
I search lunar terrain and prophesy
That winged earthlings will fly here soon
Leaving Eden footprints on the moon,
Silver trails of astronauts who must
Mold their space image in cosmic dust.
It is our generation's special boon
To decipher here the universe's rune.

Written in 1967.

CATASTROPHE TO TRIUMPH

People voicing the age-old superstition
of number 13? Did the Jinx cause
the horrible explosion in outer space?
The horrendous task of working out
safe return to earth –
Each astronaut praying in his soul
to the God of the Universe.
Perfect long distance communication
is their hope.
The earth seen as a great blue marble ball
suspended in space.

Prayers of thanksgiving
rise from the deck of the Carrier
in the Pacific.
From catastrophe to triumph!

TWO WIVES

One Astronaut's wife who does not have
the strong central support to sustain
during anguished hours of suspense
has aged within the week!
Although attending church on Sunday,
yet is shaken to the breaking point,
and looking for outer supports,
dwelling on the awful fire catastrophe
and the near tragedy of the past,
Apollo 13 explosion in outer space,
her face is the Masque of Tragedy.

The other Astronaut's wife has
the strong central support, the poise
of unshakeable Christian Faith,
faith in her loved Astronaut husband,
and in the accurate knowledge
of the expert Space Scientists
has saved her from many anguished
hours of suspense.
Faith shines through, helps loved ones,
can help the tortured wife also.

SPACE PROPHECY MADE
(1929)

I see my small son, my very own,
In the vision he is full grown
And involved in the space project,
A scientist, engrossed to protect,
Seeing flaws and solution for them,
Expert Consultant on Apollo program.

PROPHECY FULFILLED
(1969)

ARMSTRONG AND ALDRIN WALK ON MOON!
We thrill to Man's giant leap in space,
United States of America wins moon race!
T.V. shows safe return to home base.
Predestination? Son found his place,
Stretched unseen wires to the moon.
Apollo Space Project solves the rune.

CAPE KENNEDY
(1968)

Our eyes camera the heavens
focus on the speeding rocket
in Apollo's flight to the moon.
It flees myopic sight too soon.

We turn to television
on this Christmas Eve,
and hear Genesis read from pulpit
of two Astronauts in Moon orbit.

APOLLO II
(1969)

We return to our T.V. screen
to see our men float at high-noon
in heavy space accouterments:
Man's first walk on the Moon!

Rock-hounds on lunar dust
experience weightlessness in space,
suspense ends in the splashdown.
Science has won the Moon race!

With star-reaching joy I realize
My prophecy is fulfilled!

SKY-LIMNED GLORY

How long I have waited for this moment
since I prophesied many years ago
the planting of the American flag,
symbol of this free nation under God,
upon the moon, unfurled,
all fifty stars glow like Aurora
in their field of heaven's blue.
The thirteen red and white stripes
symbolize the thirteen colonies'
bravery and sacrifice.
Our flag, its glory undimmed
carried to the moon's surface by the Eagle,
symbol of freedom and endurance, now
planted by Neil Armstrong, first man
to set foot on the moon,
speaks of courage and Peace
in the emphasis of silence
on the moon's "magnificent desolation"!
Flag of the seas of earth,
whose design was born of heaven,
now beckons man to explore the cosmos.

ANTICIPATION

I lean upon the windowsill
Of anticipation,
Seeing dawn of a new day
In each sparkling golden ray,
Feeling hope for mankind
In high expectation,
Knowing God in all I view,
Dwelling in me and in you.

AMONG THE STARS

For years I wandered alone
Among the stars in space,
Now I am followed by almost
The whole human race.

ETERNAL HARMONIES

Upon the keyboard of my soul
The Master plays Eternal Harmonies,
Lifts my soul unto realms of Peace
Where love, joy and praise form melody,
Sing out, proclaim eternal verity.
Man may hear the Song of Brotherhood.
Upon the keyboard of my soul
The Master plays Eternal Harmonies.

MAN ON THE MOON

The weeping willow tree is never weaned
from Mother Earth. Are we?
At least the astronauts,
ambitious to reach the moon,
rocketed into space
and left the earth behind . . .
to return to her bosom,
after a thrilling walk on the moon!
We are children of the Earth,
fostered by the brooding Sun.

THE UNREACHABLE STAR

A man will strive to reach the highest gleam.
He tries and fails, forever trying again,
Becomes adept, achieves his dearest dream:
In distant past, a feat not dreamed by men
Of finally reaching earth's nearest moon.
Now man has climbed the golden stair to stars,
Left footprints among the meteor's rune.
The satellites that orbit Venus and Mars
Are programmed at modern cosmic science pace.
The God of Wisdom can surely uplift
A man to other planets by His Grace,
Can raise us above the densest fog drift.
We hear Spirit call "the door is ajar"
Inspiring us to aim for beacon star.

GOD'S SYMPHONY

I hear His voice in the surge of the sea.
Booming, thundering, or calm, He speaks to me,
He talks to me in the soft summer breeze,
Whispers to me in the wind in the trees.
The stars in the sky sing joyously.
I belong to God; His eternally.

Heaven and earth are mine in which to dwell.
Whispering love, roses cast a spell.
I hear His voice in the song of a bird,
The sweetest, purest music ever heard.
Only with my soul can I hear His voice
And it's only then my spirit will rejoice.

Calm and sure as the planets roll
He is speaking to my inmost soul,
Melodies and chords are truly singing,
The symphony of stars, nightly ringing
Celestial music beyond ear of men,
Heavenly strains that are above their ken.

God writes our destiny in inspired verse;
Orbiting neon spheres cannot coerce.
The planets, suns and stars obey His will.
If you listen with your soul and be still,
You will hear God's glorious symphony
And you can scale the heights of ecstasy.

BARCAROLLE OF PEACE

As we travel across the Pacific sea
Let us sing a lilting melody of Peace,
Lift our pearl-dripping oars in one release
While we steer our craft to the waiting quay.

Before us walks Jesus of Galilee.
He calms the waters, telling storms to cease.
We draw nearer the goal with every oar crease
Singing our song of Peace in jubilee.

Around and around the earth our voices ring,
Bringing love and joy from the inner soul.
Always the Brotherhood of Man is our goal,
Prophets, who strive to reveal the hidden spring.

As loving Poets, we work to cure all friction
To win the dear dream of World Peace; heart-whole,
We sing in unison Truth's uplifting barcarolle
And bring to earth love's peace-benediction.

Written on the way to the FIRST WORLD CONGRESS OF POETS, held in Manila, August 1969.

RAINBOW OF PEACE

While the silver mist of rain still falls
I see the rainbow shine upon stone walls,
Silhouette on grey veil, its colors glow
Above the white marble crosses below
Where our unknown soldier sons in rows lie
Beneath cloud-shadows of alien sky,
In the solemn quiet-cold of lonely tomb
Where acres of marble crosses like lilies bloom,
Round wheel spokes of Fort McKinley Memorial.
Their spirits, forty thousand strong, rhetorical,
Speak clearly to my clairaudient soul:
"Make Peace on Earth your burning inspired goal,
Your written word become the fertile seed,
With spoken word to conquer human greed.
Lucifer writes his signature in blood stain!
Let our great sacrifice be not in vain.
It is now yours to meet the challenge hurled.
May the rainbow of Peace arch the whole world."

SONG OF MY SOUL

A great winged bird
carried me across the ocean.
It sang the SONG OF WORLD PEACE,
most thrilling lyric I ever heard.
On the Pearl of the Pacific
I found a lotus-petaled blossom;
I called this flower Love,
breathing its rare perfume
into my soul.
I left this flower of the tropics
to grow, yet I carry the essence
wherever I go.

STONES

Sometimes a word lies heavy
heavy on the mind,
tossed by someone most unkind.
When Truth they dethrone,
will Justice ever atone?
Lies will dissipate,
in singing their own death-song
as God rights the wrong;
Truth's eternal tones vibrate
in the book of Fate.

RENDEZVOUS WITH LIFE

I find I have a rendezvous with life
On yonder emerald hill when spring is rife
And golden blossoms clothe the western slope.
I see tomorrow's dawn of certain hope;
Behold the great achievement of world peace!
This glimpse of future joy now brings release.
God's television, portrayed on soul beam,
In prophecy is part of our Lord's dream.
My psyche hears a guardian angel voice
In this Zero hour tell me to rejoice!

RAYS OF BROTHERHOOD

Like midnight sun
the orb of friendship
never sets, even in midnight hours.
It spreads golden rays
of love, brotherhood and peace,
brings needed warmth,
melts icebergs
of half-submerged hate.
Its warm glow
reaches sublime apex,
lights the way for all mankind,
colors mosaics of man's destiny.

BRIDGES

The London Bridge has crossed Atlantic Sea
We traversed this span after it came to us;
The troubles of England rode over it.
To Europe's anguished nations we gave help;
Their problems soon became ours to solve.
Just like the bridge they are sitting right here,
Not only dolls but demons and Cains came;
Assassin aliens bomb the Bridge of Love
And Compassion, staunch friendships golden link;
They would destroy the Bridge of Sustained Hope,
Constructed strongly of stones, tier on tier,
Forever spanning troubled waters of life.
Bathed in blood of Innocence, London Bridge
Becomes a sturdy symbol of lasting peace.

"IN GOD WE TRUST"

This silver coin inscribed "IN GOD WE TRUST"
is symbol of our purpose in united aims,
ideals of cosmic reach and humane scope;
eagle, insignia of freedom and talon faith.
This silver piece represents sterling strength,
the minted form portrays power of the wheel
in agriculture, industry, art and science;
Independence Hall denotes birth of a nation:
Thirteen colonies signed and declared their right
to seek happiness, likewise to free the oppressed.
This Bicentennial coin commemorates
our Nation's two hundred years of being free,
where God, justice, freedom and peace now reign
with right to work, to laugh, to love, to live.

SHARING

What I want most is something to share,
Enough to always be able to help in need,
It is ever my soulfelt, hopeful prayer.
When the heart with compassion starts to bleed
I may quickly stanch the wound with tender deed.

To share God-given gifts, knowledge, and love,
In worldly stress or more spiritual steep,
To receive graciously from Great God, where-of
No empty lives may ever make me weep,
Nor cry of a hungry child haunt my sleep.

There must always be a loaf and a hyacinth,
A lighted lamp in a firm, gentle hand,
With Faith to lead out of the labyrinth;
May I be a good Samaritan in my land,
And on through desert wastes to Samarkand!

SONG OF LOURDES

Healing waters of Lourdes murmur the song,
Whisper the fact God lives. He Lives!
High mountains echo the antiphon
Prayers of mothers with poignant tears
Answered. God lives! He lives!
Gently His wisdom speaks to man.
Through the Son, God Forgives! He forgives!
In many wonderful miracles of today,
In this sign – the Cross of Light –
Cut in the pall across the sun
Is proof Immortal God lives. He lives!

PEARLS FROM PRAYER

From seed of pain a gem has grown;
In answered prayer God's love is shown;
A jewel from extremity,
Its beauty glows eternally
Unlike the oyster doomed to die
In the scar-born pearl's extraction
We arise from pain distraction,
Counting all the prayer-born pearls.

A MIRACLE WON

It is during the sunny month of May
Dear little five year old Carla René
Lays in the Los Angeles hospital bed
With encephalitis burning her head.
Both legs and little back paralyzed,
This beautiful darling we dearly prized;
The thrust of needles in feet was not felt;
At her bed a lovely red-haired girl knelt.

The loving mother-heart filled with fear,
The worried father is standing near.
While sympathetic doctors are helpless
Knowing from experience this illness
Could be expected to end in death.
Living with prayer on every breath
Both grief-stricken parents cannot rest,
Fearing permanent paralysis at best.

Facing the fact of no treatment known,
Knowing we are not praying alone,
Turning to the Great Physician above
With the prayer of absolute faith and love,
Another mother-heart, the grandmother
Seeing God's miracle works as no other,
In love tuned in with the Creator,
Omniscient infinite Heavenly Father.

God always met us more than half-way,
In fervent prayer we seek Him each day
Knowing miracles won, keeping God's law.

I knew great joy in the vision I saw
Of dear little Carla running to me
Calling *Grandma, Grandma!* excitedly!
The child whom God saw fit to restore
Our precious Carla is normal once more.

It is a stirring experience quite rare
As God grants this heart-felt prayer.
When Carla danced at the Pomana Fair
Grandmother traveled miles to be there.
The child's little feet in rhythm of dance
In perfect beat, poised in spin and prance,
A granted miracle, proven complete
With the sight of little dancing feet!

A LAST ENCOUNTER
(Gloss on Anna Priestly's Second Encounter)

"A dark-robed stranger challenged me
His countenance was grim
But with the weapon of my youth
I met and conquered him."

Midnight, a hand clutched my throat
I could not speak or cry
But help is ever near in prayer,
My Lord was standing by.
He gently took my hand in His
Ended the fear to die.
With fear cancelled and dread stifled
In prayer I made my plea.
I clasped the stout shield of faith when
A dark-robed stranger challenged me.

When later he returned for me
In faith I took my stand
Racked with pain, by a miracle
Struck the scythe from his hand,
Reinforced by an angel band
New strength in every limb.
Returning late for another bout,
Through prayer for chance was slim
I put him completely to rout;
His countenance was grim.

Again the stranger challenged me,
With the ritual of earnest prayer

I held him off, fought gallantly.
   Returning seemed unfair,
The black-robed stranger has no ruth,
   For us he does not care.
I stand my ground with perfect faith
   And with the strength of truth
I have conquered the black-robed wraith
   With the weapon of my youth.

I met the old devil one day
   When light was growing dim,
Struck him out in the very same way,
   I keep my spirit prim
With strength won in former battles.
   I hear the Seraphim!
The fight is won for Jesus' sake,
   I keep my soul in trim,
A will that Satan cannot break,
   I met and conquered him!

MY GOD LIVES

That my GOD lives I know quite well;
I see Him shine on hill and dell;
His light glows in smile of a child,
For God is neither dead nor exiled.

In miracles of granted prayer,
I feel His Presence everywhere;
His Son uprisen, undefiled;
For God is neither dead nor exiled.

MY MOTHER'S SONG

My mother's song! I hear her sing
Through the house and garden day long.
Morning, night her rituals will ring
My mother's song!

Treasured melodies coming strong
Changing winter to breath of spring,
When other lyric voices throng
Like angel bevy carolling.
Throughout the years may God prolong
Sweetest harmony life can bring.
My mother's song!

PSALM OF THANKSGIVING

In thanking God for pain that is now past
Preceding great miracles' healing grace,
I have reached the most sublime heights at last.

Each day I seek the warmth of His embrace
And thank the Lord for love, ever Divine,
My soul has found a harbor, blessed place.

I always praise Him in my inner shrine,
And thank Him for the gift of His loved Son,
For precious healings, truths that ever shine.

It is through Jesus Christ, whose work is done
Through His sacrificial and Divine Love
Our healings granted, and great triumphs won.
We can know the grace of this Gentle Dove,
Such joy! and keep in tune with God above.

PYRAMID PROPHECY

Prophecy on pyramid's stone
Now made flesh, God's word made known,
All occurred just as He had willed,
Promise of Messiah fulfilled.

Three wise men, guided by a star
Being prophets, came from afar
On camels across desert sand
Bringing gifts to the Holyland.

Three kings star-led to the manger
Did homage to the Blessed Stranger.
Purple rank kneeled to Truth foretold,
With gifts of incense, myrrh and gold.

Songs of angels were heard on earth
Proclaiming the Messiah's birth!
He came, walked and talked among men,
Soon will appear on earth again.

His voice will be heard around the earth
Holding spellbound the whole world's girth!

NO ROOM IN THE INN

Again they thoughtlessly
   turn Him away.
Is this not the cause
   of our society's decay?
If every heart sanctuaried
   the Dear Lord
We would find the Golden Age
   with one accord.

RAYS OF WISDOM

By Wisdom raying the manger from above
the Magi found the Christ Child in haloed light.
The ways of wisdom are most pleasing
and all her paths lead to blessed peace.
May her light always shine before us,
leading our way to Brotherhood.

CHRISTMAS EVERY DAY

I long
to keep the Yule
forever green and starred,
and hope to hold the Christ in heart
all year.

MIDNIGHT CANDLE-LIGHT SERVICE

In clear and crispest frost of winter white
As air fills with dancing snowflakes of cold
The Christmas spirit wakens, joys unfold
As eyes become accustomed to softened light.
The chimes ring out the notes of *Silent Night*
To tell the greatest story ever told;
Now old familiar strains are taking hold
Of heart-memories in Yuletide delight.

With joyful Christmas Carols by church choir
In harmony we join the angel throng;
Through hymns of joyous peace to Heaven
 where-of
We find response in our soul's desire
To lend voice and wings to rapturous song
For Christ, our Messiah of selfless love.

CHRISTMAS EVE BALLAD

Remembering the stillness
  of the former Christmas Eve
The lonely old folks
  by the fireside, began to grieve.

The quiet is broken by the
  ting-a-ling of a bell.
Both of them go rushing to answer,
  each one guessing well.

The lovely face of their daughter
  with their little grandson!
With cheery laughter and singing
  a good job is done.

A Christmas tree is decorated
  and lit up in a whirl
While the smiling father holds
  the tiny baby girl.

"It is the night before Christmas
  and all through the house
Not a creature is stirring,
  not even a mouse."

While up in their beds
  their grandchildren believe
In Santa Claus coming
  on this bright Christmas Eve.

A SONG IS BORN

(High in the Alps - 1818)

Father Mohr of Obendorf, in despair
Wanted a program with the Christmas air,
Desperately worried to his very soul
Because a little mouse had chewed a hole
In his fine new Church's organ bellows;
Father was unable to face his fellows.

With no hope of any timely repairs
He sat down to compose some brand new airs.
He wrote in a very prayerful attitude.
The muse responded to his mood.
The idea germinated quite fast,
Lovely lyrics came flowing at last.

Then he called on Franz Gruber, his friend
Told about the bellows, no hope to mend.
The organist, in sympathy set to work
With only hours to solve the strange quirk.
He soon composed a haunting melody,
Angels lent their Heavenly harmony.

That night - Christmas Eve - Gruber sang the bass.
He sang with an inspired whole-souled grace.
The village high-soprano sang the lead,
A carol composed in hours met the need.
Father Mohr accompanied with guitar;
A song took hold of hearts both near and far.

The next spring the organ was all repaired,
The score for harmonizing was prepared
For the children, whose folks made gloves there.
This gave prominence to the lovely air.
They were soon asked to perform for the King.
The children joyfully travelled to sing.

Deeply impressed with its peaceful beauty
The Monarch ordered it sung as a duty
In his church for all Christmas celebrations.
Silent Night - now loved by all the nations,
A song caused by a mouse was on its way,
Now heard around the earth on Christmas Day,
    Travelled the path of Christianity
    With peace and joy to all humanity.

LEGEND OF THE CHRISTMAS ROSE

A flower's bloom
Found near the lowly manger shed
From earthly womb.

In robes of white,
It worships here the Son of God
With petaled light.

There it was said
To honor the Christ-child's birthday
Star-heralded.

CHRISTMAS MORNING

Once upon a tree a star shone bright,
Dozens of candles gave a golden light.
Soon around the pine on Christmas morning
All our excited family were gathering
In the usual custom to open gifts,
A beautiful loving group with no rifts.

Yet as I was anticipating fun
The thought came "this will be our last one.
Enjoy each minute this Christmas Day.
Another year some will be gone away."

A CHRISTMAS PRAYER

Heavenly Father:
Lift our eyes from the earth, let us not forget
the meaning of the star of Bethlehem. May we not follow
the clamor of the world but walk calmly in Thy path.
Let us keep our lamps burning brightly before us,
that shadows may recede, lighting the way for others.
Guide us all to inner peace from which Peace on Earth,
good will to all men must come, not only in the Blessed
Christmas season but every day of the year until
the whole world is at peace. Amen.

CANDLE-PINE

The odor of pine tantalizes me,
Its evergreen beauty year-round to see.
Soft and quiet are needles underfoot,
Just the spot where sleeping bags are put.
With stars overhead, green-sifted light,
A zephyr brings clean scent of woods at night,
Nostalgic dreams of one tree, a pine,
Decorated with Christmas Star-shine.
Again Dad and I tramp woods to find
A specie Candle-pine of like kind,
With perfect symmetry, dimensions right.
Its angel-topped, tinsel-draped delight!
To honor the Christ Child the tree beams.
Whispering pines still foster happy dreams.

THE CRYSTAL BALL

It's New Year! Staring into the crystal ball
To look for real happiness is true of all.
In trying to see into the whole new year,
We see again the face of one most dear.
Our happiness is made up of simple things,
Like real magic a smile from the heart brings,
In love, faith, abiding warmth of friends.
We are all searching for the very same ends,
For self-expression, a heart that always sings,
Achievement and the joy our love bewings.
The brilliant light of your loving smile
Always brightens day, makes life worth while.
Why search the world, the crystall ball?
For happiness lies within the soul's call.

JUDAS ISCARIOT
(Monologue)

"These thirty silver pieces looked big
While Satan had his hypnotic spell on me.
Now they really seem quite paltry,
A meager sum to measure Christ's worth.

I will dispose of them in the temple.
My shame shall be known around the world.
I have no hope to find a way to atone,
Despair will dwell in me forevermore.

After crucifixion Christ's wounds will heal;
My pierced conscience never will.
Is it Satan's voice I hear saying 'Kill yourself,
Go hang yourself?' Remorse is my companion.

Nothing is left for me since I betrayed
The Messiah, the Son of God.
I wish to die, to hide from Jehovah's wrath,
From the fires of Eternal Punishment!"

CROWN OF THORNS

All Heaven and earth were hushed, listening
As if to hear Almighty God's breathing;
Hearing Jesus' last words from the Cross:
"Father forgive them, they know not what they do".
The eternal challenge for me and you.

The Son of God was removed from the Cross,
In mankind's great incomparable loss.
His Divine hands and precious feet
Were unfastened from the nails of the tree
Where in torture He died for you and me.

I, Mary, lifted the crown of thorns from his brow,
Every thorn plucked from His Head then as now
From my own heart in compassion was drawn;
The drop of blood dripping from each thorn
Was duplicated from my heart, sorely torn.

All His disciples were making new vows.
From Christ's mortal agony, God endows
Christian followers with Immortal Being
Divine promise of the Holy Ghost
Fulfilled as spoken by Jesus the Host.

BURGEONING DOGWOOD

The Dogwood tree fashioned the cross;
Today it is harbinger of spring,
Of renewal of life, past hurt or loss,
Suddenly burgeoning into bloom,
Now holds song birds whose praises ring,
Forgotten cold of winter's tomb.

As Easter turns our thoughts to God;
From calvary's Cross to Resurrection,
Cross-flowered trees and blooming sod
Waft Allelujahs on Easter Day;
Man sees in Christ God's true reflection,
Since angels rolled the stones away.

TRILLIUMS

Three petals praise the Trinity
On Easter, sing of Divinity
In nature's humble mossgrown dell
Near Dogwood trees, shading it well.

Uprisen from its woodland crypt,
Pure robed in white with scented script:
Revival's message, free from art
Still can reach the recessed heart.

EASTER SUNRISE
(Grand Canyon)

From the black pit of night
The resurrection of Christ
Is portrayed in the rebirth
Of exquisite Canyon Colors;
"The heavens declare the glory of God"
With glowing sun beaming
Upon natural spires and minarets
Of God's temple of wonder,
Where antiquity of the world,
And Timeless Deity is evident
In sublime splendor of Infinite Life.
The roseate glory of the dawn
Is heralding Easter Sunday
On South Rim of the Grand Canyon.
Here reigns solemnity of awe,
Here breathes benediction of Peace;
Praising Resurrection of Christ,
"Allelulias" proclaim Eternal Life!

A MYSTIC VISION

The Savior held the Chalice to my lip;
Through spiritual sacrament in each sip
Lord Jesus shared His life, broke bread with me;
How much we need His love I can now see.
His precious sacred love has made me whole;
Revived with sustenance in food of soul,
The wine of gratitude now overflows
And washes cleanly all my earthly woes.
The life He gave is not my very own;
Is His to honor, cherish, His alone.
I hear Him saying in the midst of strife
"Lo! I am the Way, the Truth and the Life."
For He has opened wide high heaven's door
Declaring I am His forevermore.

FIFTH DIMENSION

There is a lighted Cross where I can kneel.
Beyond is one whose heavy weight I feel.
A Cross placed on top of Mt. Helix
Limns a dark shadow like the Crucifix,
Illumes fulfillment of His vast intentions.
Kneeling here I ponder His dimensions:
Below is endless depth of fractured night,
Looking up, the highest star is His height;
His breadth encircles the universe. I find
His loving arms outstretched to all mankind,
The light of God's wisdom shines eternally
Christ's Voice wings softly through infinity.
Inmost soul's divine spark looms tremendous,
The spirit of God fills endless Cosmos.
Deity is found to be immeasurable,
Unlimited Mind, the One Universal.

WONDERFUL DAY

On a glorious day
When the Lord comes again
And walks and speaks with men
Then God will have his way
On the wonderful day.

He commands and we obey.
He will clean up the earth,
Souls judged according to worth,
Destroy the devil's sway
On the wonderful day.

All who love His way
Will see the Spirit Dove;
The Lord will reign in peace and love
With no more fear alway
On the wonderful day.

Man in tune with God's lay,
Perfect harmony shall reign.
Angels join the pure refrain;
My soul will sing as they
On the wonderful day.

THANKSGIVING

Thanks be to God for sun that warms our earth,
And praise to Him for cooling summer breeze,
For star-sequined sky of infinite birth,
And beauty-gleam on snow in winter-freeze;
In spring for robin and bluebird that sings,
Give thanks to Him for autumn's color-glow,
For lovely flowers that each season brings
And flame preceding pristine powder-snow.
Thanks for lessons I learned at Mother's knee,
The blessed healing we have won through prayer,
For Christian faith that petitions reach Thee,
To know the Hand of God is everywhere:
For all our freedoms in time-tested ways
To Thee I render my Thanksgiving praise.

A GODLESS NATION?

"A Godless Nation", thoughtless folks call us!
Yet we are truly this world's first one
who year by year proclaims a Day of Thanks
for blessings and our right to worship God.
Designed in our forefather's Pilgrim mold,
respect for Freedom is enshrined in our hearts;
as descendants of early pioneers, we are
as stalwart as ageless granite hills.
A nation who pauses to thank our Father
will forever hold Liberty's torch high
to guide living sons to wisdom and truth
and light tall tapers in memory's shrine
to our soldiers who have given their lives
for our freedoms with right to worship God.

ONE NATION FOREVER

Our forefathers from across the ocean
Pioneered the way with sincere devotion
Hewed from wilderness a path in motion,
From New England to our last frontier.
With the fire of faith burning clear
Lit the torch of Liberty, ever dear.

Pilgrim founders, Fathers of our land,
Formed a nation of Christian brand,
Guided always by the Master's hand.
Two hundred years our flag has waved,
Hope of freedom: no one to be enslaved,
Citadel of Peace, on all hearts engraved.

AMERICAN HEROINE

When Mrs. Mary Hays was life's mainstay,
Hauling water to Monmouth battlefield
And earned the "Molly Pitcher" sobriquet,
Artilleryman Hays was struck without shield;
Molly tends the cannon in summer sun,
Volley on volley, the monster roars fire
Manned by Molly, stoic as a white-robed nun,
Yet never ceasing until the red-coats retire,
Like Joan of Arc, under fire, stands tall,
Arising as morning sun to light the way,
To answer freedom's urgent clarion call.
She sings with joy on Independence Day;
The soldier Molly, woman, won the fight!
Yet Mary grieves about her loss at night.

MOSAICS OF MEMORY

Across the threshold of this House of Dream
Where strong foundations are so deeply stayed,
Mosaics-memoirs – with love's glow inlaid
In pearled, enameled cloisonne's mute gleam.
The hangings are of lovely rich brocade;
Beloved design, the great master scheme;
Precisely here love spread her golden beam;
A fulfilled dream has won this accolade.
Push back today, the past to now redeem,
To see life viewed in pantomime parade . . .
Stand alert to memory's serenade.
The magic glow about me is supreme,
A minor key motif becomes heart-lace!
The vandal, Time, cannot destroy its grace.

Chained Melody Sonnet – invented by Frances Nachant.

LOTUS LILY

Petals of the lovely Lotus
Unfolding in the divine plan,
Looking upward to God and man,
Never hiding its sweet beauty,
Keeps always in line with duty.

Different is the lovely lily,
Always trusting Deity, than
A frog who moves as he can
Hopping from lily-pad to flowers,
Then to depths, where he cowers.

Each bloom shares its wealth.
Bees take the nectar for honey.
Knowing the mystic symmetry
Petaled chalice ever springing
Inspires my soul to singing.

Petals of the lotus flower
Point to various paths for man
To choose direction of his plan.
May we all decide with wisdom:
Soul's architecture at premium.

A GARDEN'S HEALING SOLACE

Pink-blossomed peach breathes consolation,
Forsythia's golden smiles are compensation;
With charming grace the birch bends low to earth,
Of sunshine and dew there is no dearth;
Carrying to the ocean hope's lost years,
The stream meanders full of splashing tears.
The sun distilled them into clouds of rain,
Returning to benign Mother Earth again,
Once more to fall on the just and unjust,
Pure and saltless they water arid dust
Into a gay blooming fragrant bower,
Where God smiles with each lovely flower.
Teardrops that formerly streamed down my face,
Fostered deep compassion for the human race.
Of Mercy, Faith dwells where red roses grow
With sweet Hope enflamed bright as heaven's glow.

GOLDEN RAIN

Today it's raining golden daffodils
By murmuring brooks and slow flowing rills
Mother Nature is getting out her frills.

She gayly primps and paints her tulips red
With cheerful color-riot in each bed
They are all prettily bediamonded.

With promise of gold from plantings of fall
Her moods are not being dampened at all,
Are growing brighter with each robin's call.

She wakens all the daffodils from sleep,
Will soon be in color of gold knee-deep.
The sun-brightened skies are ceasing to weep.

All earth awake, birds winging from the hills,
Again it's spring and Mother Nature thrills
With all her golden swaying daffodils.

THE GREATEST POET

In mending souls and bringing forth the truth,
Beatitudes, inspired, form a flowing fount;
The Son of God used words so filled with ruth
And wrought them into Sermon on the mount.
The parable called "Pearl Without A Price"
Is a lovely, apt, compressed similitude;
His fire is selfless love that thaws the ice,
The highest muse persuades creative mood.

The Lord's Own Prayer is now a joyful song,
The greatest lyric under faithful sun,
In singing, Lo! I hear the angel throng;
Dramatic Poet! His imagery won.
He spoke with moving force and graphic span
In zealous passion: Rays of God to man.

THERAPY IN POETRY

The heavy-weighted mind can still take wing,
In fancy's dream of high poetic flight
Can soar above every mundane thing
In rhythmic beat and lyric sweet delight;
For even saddest hearts can learn to glow
As worldly problems quietly steal away;
No matter if chilly rains and winds do blow
At close of any weary, trying day.

From all the neatly gleaned and golden sheaves,
Inspired Beatitudes and sacred psalms,
And tender heart-release between the leaves,
The comfort brings a peace from all your qualms;
In fever, swifter healing, blessed calm
Is found in magic of Twenty-third Psalm.

POETRY IS . . .

A dew-drop's pose on petal of a rose
Leaves breathing heart throes, a song in repose;
At dawn its bird-song, the Cathedral gong;
A garden's fresh ground where healing is found;

To mother, truly the babe on her knee,
The smile of a child, a faun in the wild,
Carillons at twilight, a prayer at night,
Carols Christmas Eve, great tales to believe;

Treasured book-friends, life's great amends,
Solace in sorrow, dawn of tomorrow;
Song of the sea, west winds melody,
Star-pointing trees, song on mountain breeze.

It is everything in the songs we sing,
Soul music, euphony, and heavenly harmony.

CATHEDRAL SPIRES

Myriad star's delicate tracery,
Silver of crescent moon-jewels light
Silhouette against night's soft velvet;
Comes a flame of inspirational fire,
We see the lighted Cathedral spire,
Beacon pointing heavenward,
Guiding us through darkness of night.

POETRY IS FIRE MELTING ICE

Poetry is bleeding from the soul,
Sometimes it is weeping from the heart
Or song of rejoicing ecstasy;
It is fire melting ice,
Is seeing beyond the physical,
Hearing music above the din,
Is prophesying beyond the day,
Is looking within, height and depth,
Outward into the magnitude of infinity;
Reaching for a star and finding God.

POET AND THE WORD

He turns the word
as if it were a jewel,
a fiery opal,
to catch the fire,
the gleam of the eternal flame
of inspiration,
until his heart and pen ignite.

HEALING WATERS

Here find healing waters of poetry
the pure flowing fountain
at the shrine in the garden of love
flowing effervescing wine.
All who pass this way
may quench their thirst.
Around the basin brim
are fragrant white lilies.
Rest here and refresh your spirit
in beauty and in peace.

I TOUCHED A STAR

I reached for God and touched a star!
Then reached for a star and found God!
Nevermore will He seem so far.
I reached for God and touched a star,
Finding unity singular.
Omnipotence springs from the sod,
I reached for God and touched a star
Then reached for a star and found God!

THE TREASURE HUNT

I have found my way to Happy Retreat,
  It is there for him who hath
Turned from the freeway of Self-Deceit
  To the right, up Duty's Path.

You will not weary or go wrong.
  Treasure field, I must confess,
Is on a road quite straight and long,
  The highway called Unselfishness.

THE AFTERGLOW

When the skies are black as thunder
And sorrow gets you down under
Although tears may be as quicklime
You are coming up for the third time
Buoyant spirit will rise again
Winging above the foamy main
Breathing a prayer lifts above woe
Realizing Faith's Blessed afterglow

HARMONY

True friendship, thoughts in blend,
Melodious tones of golden sound,
Diapason, concord without end,
Harmonies in cadence quite profound
From the Prelude to Grand Finale
When the Maestro rings the curtain down
Sweet music wraps us around and around.

AWARENESS

Awareness of God is felt near the sea,
Magnitude mirrors cosmic master-key.
His power in buoyancy floats iron hull,
Is cradling after the fierce storm's lull,
Is eternal rhythm of moon-tide mystery,
Is crash and roar of breakers; His artistry:
Backdrop of blue, white spray upon rocks,
Blind faith of winging airborne flocks;
Love reflects on water in sunbeam glisten,
In myriad forms of life: His provision.
Man tills the soil; God tends ocean bed
Where men garner a very sumptuous spread.

Man's waste increases dire consequence
Of depending more upon the sea for sustenance!
From the sea the sun draws mist into a cloud,
To refresh earth it falls in snow to enshroud
Mountain Peak, becomes a fresh reservoir.
All life depends on this cycle evermore.
Ocean's great power can claim or sustain.
The sea spells freedom or it can enchain.
Astronauts, cradled by waves, returning to base,
By splashdown were saved to win the moon race!
As each raindrop returns to the sea's immensity
Each soul must return to the Absolute eventually!

STAINED-GLASS WINDOWS

With stained-glass windows of sunset
Lighting altars of reverent prayer,
Thanks for blessings we cannot forget,
As in humble spirit we kneel there,
All Earth is the cathedral floor
On mountain, valley, or seashore;
Space reaching trees, pointing spire
Shelter loft of invisible choir;
The star-jewelled sky is its dome:
Our prayers reach Him abroad or home.

On the deck of the sinking ship
We each pray from our inner soul
Not just with service of the lip,
As the frightening billows roll
No chance to find a man built church
When high seas swing a rolling lurch.
In the airplane when storms arise
He hears our apprehensive cries;
We renew our soul's faith in prayer:
Omnipotent God is everywhere!

HOMING PIGEONS

(To My Son Grant)

Those letters you wrote from
No-man's-land
From the waste paper basket
pull my hand.
The pigeon-holes were made
for homing birds.
How can I destroy a heart's
own words?
To clear a desk must be
a special art
Like sweeping out the corners
of my heart.

BLUE VIOLETS

"Let us go down to the stream
under the willow tree.
Are the violets out?"
Hear the excited scream
"I found a blue one! See!"
The children loudly shout.
No lovelier flowers than they,
Children in my garden in May.

FLOWER OF HEAVEN
(To Trudy)

Fragrant breath of an angel; sweet
Tiny tendril fingers, doll feet;
Snuggle down, cuddled in my arms
As I sing lullabies to your charms.

Smile of God, in my joy and mirth,
Fun and laughter came with your birth,
Mine to hold, to love, to cherish,
Mother's love will never perish.
You are dearly loved; as the moon beams
Angels hover near to guard your dreams.

VOICES OF CHERUBIM

(To Joyce)

Let my baby always sing
Her tinkling laughter ever ring
The light of her turquoise eyes
Unrivaled by summer skies.

When I am sad and to her cling
My Joy-Carol will always sing.
May life be kind in years after
No grief to quell happy laughter.

When this child starts to vocalize
Cherubim come to harmonize.
Such love, joy and lilt she brings.
I pray my baby always sings.

FLIGHT OF THE LAST FLEDGLING

Leaving me quite alone on this lovely day
The last of my fledglings has flown away.
Suddenly the air is bereft of song!
Lovingly, faithfully, for her I pray.

Though she left with regretful farewell to me,
Her heart fills with happy thrilled expectancy,
Perching in safety on the shoulder of God,
Or nestled in His arms most tenderly.

God has but loaned me the all precious prize
Winging on to build a nest quite Eden-wise.

PORTRAIT OF FATHER

One little, two little, three little girls
Bright-eyed pixie, and one with dark curls
Sitting on his knee with a brown-eyed blond;
Our Daddy of whom we were so very fond,
In the old Colonial rocking chair
As he gently rocked he sang to us there.

The stories he had lived, told and retold
Of many and varied adventures so bold,
About brave soldiers and Custer's Massacre,
In pageantry of his life as it did occur;
Of Indian Scouts and Buffalo Bill;
Chief Sitting Bull's most stubborn will.

Dad's love for his Cavalry horse we felt,
And his fondness for Teddy Roosevelt,
Exploits of his Rough Riders he would tell;
Of swamps, now the great Panama Canal
Where he caught malaria and never got well!
Yankee with cotton plantations to sell!

Dad told of the landing on Plymouth Rock,
Of our own ancestral Pilgrim stock;
Of vivisection at Rush Medical College
Where he studied to acquire knowledge;
His soul rebelled at the sight and sounds,
Creatures suffering as memory rebounds.

Father was always first to help in distress,
A great many persons his soul did bless.

Putting himself last all of the time,
Such unselfishness finds no words in rhyme.

Eyes twinkling with humor, you can believe
A good Irish story was up his sleeve.
Great poems he recited, some he wrote
Always to mother in most loving note;
Of Cousin Edward Fitzgerald's name
Whose translation of "Rubaiyat" won fame.

On the wall a West Point portrait was hung
Another American patriot unsung,
Handsome, debonair, with sword at his side;
"The picture is our Dad", we point with pride.

Father's prediction was we would some day
Be compelled to whip the Japs!
His singing of army songs, Reveille
then Taps . . . .

MOTHER

I see the love light in your smiling eyes,
Illuminating glow as from a sunrise,
Your lovely tapered hands I clearly see,
Those tender ones that did so much for me.
I feel them tenderly caress me now,
The cool touch upon my fevered brow.

I see your face in the flowers I bring
And hear your voice in sacred songs I sing,
The joy of music in tunes we harmonized,
Remembrance that is now quite deeply prized.
Even today I feel your fond embrace,
Beautiful vision in satin and lace.

How many times you kissed my tear stained face,
Guided my footsteps in the way of grace,
Treated those bruised shins, scrubbed my ears,
Comforted my heart and quelled my fears.
God's gift to the world is mother-love,
Gracious little mother in Heaven above.

The door of Heaven opened; its song swells.
Your guardian-angel presence now tells
In the softest voice of an angel's breath,
Your immortal soul proves Christ conquered death.

PORTRAIT OF GREAT GRANDMOTHER

Grandmother's corset was put on tightly laced
Until she became really quite red-faced
With the tussle on the girdle, cinched in,
To help make her look very neat and thin.

She rushed to adjust the quilted bustle
And taffeta petticoat with its rustle;
Now the blue satin dress, then a big hat,
With white ostrich plumes draped over that.

A dash of perfume made her smell flower sweet,
Long skirts were swishing around her small feet.
Grandmother was looking pert and discreet
As her bustle moved in rhythm down the street.

PROPHETIC VISION

(New San Diego, California – 1867)

Alonzo Horton seeing a vision dream,
Was led to found a city on this spot.
Foresight impelled him to work out a scheme
In fairest climate with very careful thought;
Then petty rivals clouded heaven's beam.
Old Town jealousy built a counter-plot;
Opposing winds fanned Horton's self-esteem.
He planned to give each home-builder a lot.
The flame of lighted torch soon wrought a thaw.
Determination fostered his fine plan
And won all the land-title suits at law;
Persuasion finally won the old clan.
He founded a city called "Heaven-on-Earth";
Now prophet Horton's vision proves of worth.

COLLAGE OF MEMORY

This heirloom patchwork quilt
  is a collage of memory,
Finely stitched by love and good
  old-fashioned industry.

From unforgettable bygone days
  all pieced together
By the adhesive of love, joy, grief
  in life's uncertain weather.

This pattern is bringing back certain
  happy childhood days;
My loved doll's quilt has many such
  love-feather-stitched arrays.

This small piece is dear mother's
  lovely satin wedding gown;
This one a dress she wore on days
  she went shopping down-town.

The blue block was the formal
  I wore to the Junior Prom.
It was quite lovely, elegant, and it
  was sewn by my loved Mom.

As I wrap the treasured quilt close
  about me like a glove
I feel the cozy, cuddly warmth
  of Grandmother's love.

THE QUEEN

The same constellations are overhead,
The old pale moon still shines upon my bed.
Ursa Major and North Star followed me
To Southern California's temperate clime
Where I am putting nostalgia into rhyme.

My thoughts are winging away back home,
To purple-gold sunsets, never monochrome,
While golden mosaics on Elliot Bay fall.
In dreamy witching hour's twilight spell
My mind turns to things remembered well.

Cerulean lakes, trees of richest green
Standing like sentinels, guarding the Queen;
Music of the world's greatest Carillons;
Science building with scintillating fountains;
Mt. Rainier, most beautiful of mountains.

Tallest Space Needle pointing to the skies,
As our Scientific achievements most wise,
Point prophetically to a future day
When long-distance message to the stars
Will be echoed back from the Moon and Mars.

White sails on Lake Washington; Cascade range
Breathing of mysterious history quite strange;
The floating bridge with rows of topaz lights,
Dazzling mirrored jewels flashing at night,
Is a lovely unforgettable sight.

Waiting for you with warmly open arms
The Queen awaits you with her special charms,
Her warm heart beat, like the roll of the drum
Stirs you as the pageantry moves along,
Wooing the soul of a poet to song.

She has come through fire to rise again,
Through vision of stalwart women and men
Set in gardens of heavenly beauty,
Rhododendrons, azalea and roses
In colorful, gorgeous bloom she poses.

At eve, seen in purple robe and crown of gold
Painted from God's palette, is sight to behold!
The queen whose beauty has never been told,
In King Winter's Cavalcade wearing ermine robe,
Reigns as fairest Beauty Queen of the globe.

Note: Written in 1961, recited on Radio Station KBBW in 1964.

DR. ALBERT SWEITZER'S MADRIGAL

I think that God had played on his heart-strings
The song of tender, pure compassion-love
Attuned to saints and archangels there-of
Inspired three souls to join the song he sings.

He holds the pitch while pains deep moan still rings.
Like gentle light on breast of brooding dove,
Those blessed and healing, praying hands, where-of
His touch is like the brush of angel wings.

He routed dread disease, a haunting wraith!
With Holy Passion his life is replete;
The classic wrought could fill an endless tome,
Composed compassion's Madrigal of faith:
With music, charm, and love the pages beat.
The Cosmic choir sweetly sang him home!

THE NIGHTINGALE

I hear the nightingale singing.
Its lovely dulcet tones
Are pleasing to my ear;
Above this another tune is ringing,
A song the wounded hear,
Hymn of compassionate love;
When time blots all notes from its pages
The song of Florence Nightingale
Will echo down the corridors of ages.

WINGS

Does Creator God love us less
Than the lowly caterpillar?
Will he also create for us
Shimmering wings of gossamer?
Angels, dropping here a prayer
And a loving blessing there?
Not just glorious dreams at night
But wings to fly in full sunlight.

ANOTHER JUDAS

A Judas left a shadow stain on high,
Without human kindness, with lethal craft
He planned an honored statesman's day to die,
Left the White House door ajar to crime's draft.
For cash he schemed to meet the deadline date,
Sirhan accomplished it, the crowd agape!
With greed and spite in cruel plans of hate,
In stolen car he planned to make escape;
He robbed the nation of one prepared to lead,
Erased Robert's name from elect to be,
Who stood for justice, peace and human need;
A trustworthy statesman, with E.S.P.,
A leader, a Lincoln, lost in his prime!
All Satan's devils labor overtime.

APOSTROPHE TO BEETHOVEN

As huge glaciers have carved in granite
the famed El Capitan in Yosemite Valley
Your magnificent music compositions,
were formed by suffering and emotional pressure,
ignited by the divine spark of creative genius.
Enthralled we listen, filled with wonder,
hearing mountains echo the antiphon.
You left us an immortal legacy!

BACH'S MUSIC

Bach's pure music, voice of mystery,
awakens the psyche,
heralding us to ascend to higher plane.
In refining atmosphere
finding refreshing dew
of ethereal distillation cleansing
earthly dross, bathing us
in golden light of spiritual joy
where the soul tunes with the rhythm
of singing stars.

THE MASTER'S HAND

The cymbals of brass strike a rhythmic beat,
Yet the heart and soul need Heaven's heat.
Music can shut all pangs of sorrow out,
Or tune the heart-strings until they are taut;
The bow drawn by a capricious demigod
Can ache the air with the most poignant prod.

The Master plays with such caressing skill
Until my soul drinks of wine its fill
Of pathos so poignantly sweet and sad,
Then surfeited, suddenly becomes glad;
Warm golden dreams again awake in my breast
All the blithesome sorrow of love's unrest.

Thus magnetized, I hug them to my heart,
Old melodies give memory a start,
Love leans from the high casement and smiles
While newer songs of love my heart beguiles
And one's soul sings with the violin,
A high heaven music lovers enter in.

HARBOR OF ART

Who can contemplate a shell's
   pearled beauty, so exquisite
And not acknowledge the traces
   of Divine Art upon it?
Did the Great Artist linger
   on the seashore and dream
Of planting the waters with works
   of Art to such extreme,
In myriad sculptured designs
   with color pigment invested,
When on the Seventh Day He rested?

Architect of the universe engraved
   the signature of the Creator
On Double Sunrise, Moon Scallops,
   in design on the Sand Dollar,
And on trumpeter Triton's Horn,
   on purple splurge of the urchin
And Sea-pansy's delicate turn,
   the Pearled Nautilus, with rainbow
On Pearly cirrus clouds drawn;
   Queen's Pink Conch orchestrating
Aeolian winds and picturing dawn;
   the rare Harp and Imperial Volute,
All this in seas man will pollute.

MUSIC OF THE SOUL

A smile is music sung right from the soul.
It wings the heart along our earthly flight,
Swifter than words, winging on beam of light,
Pure melody written on heaven's scroll.

On dark waters, with ringing barcarolle,
It forms a beacon for our inner sight;
A smile is music sung right from the soul,
It wings the heart along our earthly flight.

Smiles waken faith, a power to console
When hope is dulled by sky no longer bright,
It lifts us to Harmony's golden height
Where we can feel Divine Love in control.
A smile is music sung right from the soul,
It wings the heart along our earthly flight.

AEOLIAN HARP

The soft winds of love
Flow over my heart,
Lean against silence;
Then murmur your name
And sweep the strings to song.

KEYBOARD OF THE WIND

I hear the Song of Loneliness
Played upon the keyboard of the wind.
In shadows of lost evenings
I see your beautiful face limned.
Oh to transpose the minor strain
To love's high ecstasy again.

LOVE'S MUSIC

He called me his Darling today,
Now my heart is singing again,
Gone is shadow of doubt and pain,
As courage and joy come to me,
Hoping my heart-wish soon will be.

Many have called me darling or dear,
Never bringing such thrill before,
I feel like singing forevermore!
To make him happy too is my goal,
Who brings forth the music of my soul.

MY HARP – THE LOOM

My harp – the loom on which I weave my dreams,
The woven cloth, in threads of rose and gold,
These hands are weaving. Memory's brilliant scenes
Are pageant portraits on the vibrant strings,
In golden themes of music's soothing air.
A lovely vision is reviewed once more,
Renewed by only soft caressing hands,
The face, the Dearest One, the sweetest songs
Of early days, recalling young love's thrill,
A tune revealing magic-carpet-joy
To carry us to fair Enchanted Land;
Of living happy days enthralled again;
Now spinning dreams of visions rare delight,
I see Eternal Hope arise to life.

TAKE TIME

Take time to think . . .
  it is a source of power.

Take time to work . . .
  it is the price of success.

Take time to read . . .
  it is the fountain of wisdom.

Take time to love and be loved . . .
  it is a God-given privilege.

Take time to be friendly . . .
  it is the road to happiness.

Take time to smile . . .
  it is music of the soul.

Take time to laugh . . .
  it is a lift for the spirit.

Take time to dream, to meditate . . .
  it fosters creative inspiration.

Take time to express gratitude . . .
  it is a virtue.

Take time to share . . .
  "it is more blessed to give".

Take time to worship . . .
 it is the soul's great need.

Take time to thank God . . .
 it is from Him all blessings flow.

Take time to pray . . .
 it is the greatest source of power.

SOUL ATTRIBUTES

I looked into his eyes
For attributes I highly prize
And wondered if he had a soul.
His expression was very droll.
Brown eyes looked into mine closely.
I saw affection, loyalty,
Trustworthiness, intelligence,
Faithfulness, faith, and patience.
He plainly shows his gratitude,
Faithful pal of my solitude.
To express joy, he does not fail,
Playful greeting in wagging tail.

He followed me, obeyed commands,
Gently licked my tears, my hands;
His sympathy, so tenderly shown;
A truer friend I have never known.
His watchfulness, and memory,
Such loyal love and empathy;
Each of these a soul attribute
Although called a dumb brute.
In my dog's endearing ways
He taught me for many long days;
In his pathetic eyes I see
How God has answered me.

EXTRA-SENSORY PERCEPTION

Blackie, the engineer's dog
ran to meet the train
on schedule each day
to greet his master.
Thus watchless ones knew the hour
although far from watchtower.
The day his master died
Blackie ceased meeting the train . . .
He bowed to final curtain.

REINCARNATION

Today the French poodle had a ten dollar trim
So my hair was cut around a china bowl's rim.
My wifey skipped her beauty salon appointment;
Then shampooed her hair with appropriate intent.

Really enough to drive a mere man to court.
For when I decide to rest on the davenport
That bediamonded poodle is there for a nap,
Any other time, tenderly cuddled on her lap.

Mitzi rules this castle like a royal queen.
Such a soft and pampered life I have never seen!
If there is a reincarnated state of being
I will come back a toy poodle, tail agleeing!

GIANT PSYCHOTIC

The sea, tempestuous, angry, tossing ships about.
Great vessels, rolled by a giant psychotic;
the mountainous waters reach pinnacles, clutch, recede
into deepest troughs, pitched high and low to destroy.
My mind is like the ship in the tempest of life,
rising to heights, then down to the depths,
from ecstasy to frustration and fury.
Against my heart the maelstrom crescendos;
caught in a black hour's unmerciful storm . . .
With the dawn comes sunshine on the ocean,
calm yet with an eternal restlessness
like a soul making peace with God.

IMMORTAL SCULPTOR

In Red Rock Valley we pause
before the works of God,
Bell Mountain then Little Chapel
facing the monument of Virgin Mary,
holding the Christ Child,
clothed in roseate beauty
of sun-kissed color,
sculptured by the Immortal Sculptor.
Nature says "Come rest, be refreshed."
God's law of beauty in color
reigns supreme in this land
of peace and inspiration
where artists paint, writers pause,
poets sing until hills echo
their song of praise.
How can man deny God when His Works
speak so eloquently?

CLIFF-DWELLERS, A.D. 1000

Ancient Cliff-Dwellers of Mesa Verde, Colorado,
Whose stone castles show Pueblo Indians' bravado,
Built many centuries before Columbus was alive,
Were America's only royalty; hoping to survive
They held court around the council fires;
Co-operation was the secret that inspires.
Looking down from high turrets so sheer
Ladders pulled up, rising above all fear,
Finding sweet serene repose
Our insomnia hardly knows.

For these patient builders of the past
With their mummies petrified to last,
And the mortar, trowels and tripods,
With their superstitions and their gods,
We feel appreciation and empathy
For their bequest of herb pharmacy
And contributions to husbandry.
Here is mystery and fascination
In contemplative rumination.
Did their chiefs and their sages
Looking forward down the ages
Within the Garden-of-the-Gods,
From their prophets, hear the warning
Today's rebel sons are scorning?

TEMPLES OF MANITO

From Fire-falls, at Glacier Point
Yosemite Valley,
We gather live sparks falling
from the wand of a fairy.
Summer zephyrs are fanning flames
to heart-warming glow
Where red-orange fire-falls drop
to one thousand feet below.

Indian Love Call ringing clearly
brings heart-throe.
Listen! From hill to hill ululating
notes sing to and fro.
Comes answering voices of her lover
young Golden-Bow;
Long parted, they seek each other
in temples of Manito.

Note: Indian legends name Manito as God of Nature.

SENTINELS ON THE NAVAJO TRAIL

On the Mojave Desert Saguaro stand
Stiffly stoic and stern, guarding the land,
Braves left their homes on the Navajo trail
Wind and sand flail their bones.

The spirit of the proud Navajo Chief
Once filled with grief for his starved tribe,
Now sees prosperity's promising sign
In the tribe's productive uranium mine.

Since Providence confirms native belief,
Will the old Chief's soul now find relief?

PORTRAIT OF AN OLD MAN

As the old man recalls the past
his face, montage of moving moods,
sun or cloud-shadowed with grief,
harvests scorn, pity, hope, regret
or light of love, mirth, joy,
kaleidoscope of life's true worth.
We read scenes, he hears sounds,
tape-recorded on memory.
Faith in Christ lights his face.

AUBADE

This Pandora's box opened at dawn today.
Out came the gift of Time, a whole new now!
Before form, Time was, yet is born anew.
The years etch cameos for us in array.
Time was . . . before the Creator would endow
The world with light and moon-silver dew.

Although now is forever, today is prime,
Yours to use wisely, not squander, but how?
Time reaches far beyond the distant view.
Image of Eternity is a collage of time.
Today is a gift to you.

DESERT PSALM

Not only the rose lifts its heart to God.
The desert cactus blooms from arid clod
And Yucca candles grace the altar too
While Ocotilla lights a flame for you.
The Joshua tree lifts two arms in prayer
Sajauro give their annual offering there,
And varied species brilliant cacti bloom
Are censers burning rare scents to perfume.

The Century plant holds sacrifice outstretched,
In balmy desert twilight-mauve is etched;
Verbena, kneeling, is resigned to fate,
Here each is praising God in special state.
Birds in full choir their sweet voices raise
And organ-pipes waft up their song of praise.

FLOWERING PEACE

In my garden
today I found a rosebud!
Pink edges each petal,
heralds dawn of peace,
unfolds heart of gold
to choir of angels.
Petals of the Rose of Peace
grow larger, larger,
spread, become a canopy
over all the earth.

CLOISTERED MONK

In fall the mountain monk,
white-cowled, stalwart, with storm
clouding his face,
echoes thunder of Sinai and Calvary,
in spring wears a cirrus halo
while choir of birds
sing heavenly hymns.

PINK-PETALED SYMPHONY OF SPRING

Pink-petaled symphony rings clear.
We stop to breathe the perfume here.
Choired melodies sprightly ring
When feathered throats begin to sing.
Arpeggiod ecstasy brings cheer.

We look for their return each year,
Trilling cadenzas, always dear!
This is the certain sign of spring
Pink-petaled symphony!

Orioles serenade my ear
While mocking birds in tune appear.
With the blossoms, April days bring
Celestial anthems for the King,
Now heard upon this earthly sphere:
Pink-petaled symphony!

THE FOUNTAIN

A young man travelled this earth
In search of perpetuity of youth.
He greatly longed to find the truth.
He spent his time, his strength and gold
Seeking means to never grow old.

One night a vision did impress.
He dreamed an angel came and spoke:
"Halt here! The secret to evoke
Is within your innermost soul.
Look to do good, make it your goal."

Thomas remembered his dream.
With bright morning sun he awoke!
He never forgot the angel who spoke:
"Console those who grieve; as you grow
The sweet fountain will flow!"

A little boy was orphaned by war;
His mother passed on about then;
Tom gave him love and a home again.
When a neighbor was ill, he took heed,
Each day he found someone in need.

Although he managed most politic
They flocked to him like a bishopric.
He helped the hungry, the blind, the sick.
Then the rich man who lived on the hill
Left him all he owned in his will.

The miserly called him "stark mad",
The hard, the practical said "quite foolish"
Thinking this course would impoverish.
The compassionate ones called him saint,
His radiant face a Raphael should paint!

MY RAPTURED WISH

My wishing well was full of tears.
There is miracle in rites God hears.
He changed the salty specimen
Into Faith's fresh-flowing fountain.

Through shining love and gold of prayer
There is life-giving water to share.
Gratitude-minted, these coins I throw
Cause the waters to overflow.

A SILKEN SEINE

Houseman had no net to capture
  The sunset from the main
Or hold the dawn until it comes again;
  But I have a sturdy seine,
The silken net of memory
  Holds the dawn until it is freed
When the glory of a new day
  Will really exceed.
My golden seine holds color mosaics
  Of sky and sea,
Captured living, glowing trochaics
  For you and me.

PAGES OF AN OLD BOOK

I love the ancient, out of print
most reverently used tomes
With their margin notes like
helpful little gnomes.

Along the borders are prints
of little Elfin shoes;
I am captured within four walls
unheeding of this ruse.

Led by invisible gently firm
little pixie hands
I follow them into gates opening
into fairylands.

Where aesthetic wonders captivate,
charm and amuse
Nightingales are singing to me
without price or dues.

WAS I A STONE?

"From dust Jehovah created man,
He breathed into man a soul."

Stones disintegrate into atoms, molecules,
sand and soil to feed plants.
From disintegration to integration
stones are my food.
Earth is a stone swinging in space.
God's plan is a cycle of change
of conservation, economy in creation.
Mobility of the human body is miracle.
Animating mind only God can explain.
Within the stone He locked a great secret.
Within the soul He locked a greater secret.
Darwin traced his origin back to apes,
I trace my origin back to stone.

MAHATMA GHANDI'S BLOODLESS REVOLUTION

Salute to the great Mahatma Ghandi!
A man who lived his Christianity!
He stood alone in pure unselfishness –
A martyr to India's cause! No less.

In this epic a new order had begun,
A nation's independence sanely won;
Through supplication and with sacrifice
His high ideals and faith thawed the ice.

The cherished company of his family
Was sacrificed by the Zealot Ghandi
To study at Oxford in England to learn
To know and understand those who govern.

His own spiritual qualification
Shows the true signs of predestination,
He pursued his studies with loneliness,
And achieved all the great rewards that bless.

A man with spiritual power to assure,
A true prophet willing to endure,
With devotion, fasted in white-robed faith
Until he soon became almost a wraith.

With determination to win a bloodless strife
And willingness to lay down his precious life
To liberate his loved, oppressed nation
He steadfastly refused to eat the ration.

Believing, teaching passive resistance,
India's loved leader covered the distance.
His countenance was growing pretty wan
But Heaven gave him strength to carry on.

When officers of the great British Empire
Locked him in a cell, his need was dire;
In the attempt to force him to break the fast
To save his life; Ghandi's prayers won at last!

They broke all opposition to Mahatma's plea
For all his loved country to be set free.
He proved to be a truly great example
That passive resistance does not trample.

Love held his people under good control.
The followers kept a vigilance of soul
With such strict and loving obedience
To their Leader, who opposed violence.

Ghandi, through invocation, accomplished
A task most men would have soon relinquished,
One that no ordinary man could finish.
Through perseverance he won his soul's wish.

Great contrast to the French Revolution
By violence from under oppression won;
The bloody horrors of a freedom grasped
By cruel terror method was unsurpassed.

In Russia's revolution of violence
The Iron Curtain hid terror intense;

Mexico was for years in upheaval,
Shots in the midst of Fiesta revel.

Chinese nation was divided gory red,
At Valley Forge our soldiers' blood was shed,
Bright red stains on white of winter's snow
As bitterest cutting north winds blow.

No blood on Ghandi's robe of purest white,
His saintly hands clasped in prayer every night.
India's cause was won through unselfed love,
In entreaty to our Father above.

He refused to obey laws quite unjust,
Held passive resistance to be a must;
Consistently turning the other cheek,
He proved the strength of the gentle and meek.

A world had waited with abated breath
In fear the Mahatma would starve to death.
Little emaciated Ghandi was blessed.
The great British Empire had acquiesced!

Full honors to a noble soul of worth!
India's leader showed this war torn earth
The miracle way to win lasting peace;
First bloodless revolution, that war cease.

A peace won to last we hope forever
That fosters and builds human endeavor;
Ghandi led India toward literacy
Out of oppression and stark poverty.

With the outgrown caste system broken down
Every child will wear a princely crown
Of jewels of Hope, Faith and God's Love,
Lighted by a star from Heaven above.

Mahatma Ghandi embraced Christ Jesus
Whose perfect love has power to lift us
Above all types of painful human woe
By the power of Divine Love the saints know.

All the civilized nations loved Ghandi,
Heart of unselfed love – the epitome –
He did all one compassionate soul can
In fostering the Brotherhood of Man.

He was assassinated by his own countryman
Who surely was not a strictly sane one.
May the world long remember revered Ghandi,
Martyred in the great cause of Liberty.

THE WIND AND GOD

God, always invisible, in benign wind,
Moves masses of clouds for baptism of rain,
Cleanses, disperses heavy polluted air,
Lifts helicopter to save a life chance thinned,
While supporting wings of jet airplane,
And blows away blind fog for days more fair.

Wind wafts the singing lark and winged seed,
Pollenizes flowers, fruit, corn and grain.
Of summer breezes nature is aware.
In attar of roses, honey bees feed.
    Invisible Love is there!

INSTIGATOR OF CLOCKS

Sun! Instigator of alarm clocks
In casting tall shadows from mountain height
Is influential in creating the sun dial.
Winter froze water-time to crystal rocks,
Rendered useless until Spring's golden light
Turned leaves in life's book . . . no denial!

Yet earth's turning, turning, day by day,
Controls brakes on Sun's scorching blight,
Measures time: day and night without trial;
Moon axis turns with deliberate delay:
Time in God's vial.

CARILLONS

Carillons at noon
are heard by us hospital patients,
prisoners of pain,
bathing us in a flow of tranquillity.
In the concert from the bell-tower
of St. James,
Music! gentle rain upon a desert.
August heat becomes April promise.

MOMENT OF DELIGHT

Although lighter than thistledown
spontaneous kiss
blown from a loving baby-girl's hand
reaches the heart.

INSOMNIA

Insomnia, with plicatured wings
perches on my pillow.
Poe's raven quotes "Nevermore",
Five A.M. dawns . . .
Eyelashes are webbed in sleep.
Six A.M. alarm rings.

SAN DIEGO MISSION DE ALCALA

(July 16, 1769)

At chosen mission site, now called Old Town,
With halo-glow, fire of burning zeal,
Father Serra planted the Cross and Crown;
To light paths, broke ground to piously kneel;
Established missions along the Gold Coast.
The Spanish Crown furnished soldier escorts.
In solemn fervor Serra held the Host,
Then trekked on northward, building mission ports.

A blazing fire lit the starless sky,
Father Jaime, in blood-stained clothes was found;
Profaned by native thieves, padres decry!
Padre Serra declared this hallowed ground.
The first California Mission was razed!
The rebuilt mission prospered, God be praised!

OLD MISSION
SAN JUAN CAPISTRANO, CALIFORNIA

The pure white doves beside the flower bed
Welcome with message of love by Padre led.
They strut about the ancient mission ground
As Padres on retreat they make their round.

In reverence they perch near arch-framed bells,
Whose daily ringing, God's clear message tells.
They flock at Father Serra statue's fulcrum
In poinsettia-graced niche of Christ's Kingdom.

March proclaims Fiesta of Swallows Return.
While many red cathedral candles burn
The chapel, with its gold Spanish altar
Surviving earthquake, still holds the Psalter!

Compassionate St. Francis walks this place,
We sense the touch of celestial embrace.

IN SANTA BARBARA MISSION

As chiming bells from mission towers proclaim
Repairs of quake-damaged walls are complete,
A widow, shattered by sorrow's prone defeat,
Now finds the Chapel of Serra's last aim.
Still young, a trembling Aspen leaf, she came
To find inside the door that peace is replete;
Black-robed priests devoutly kneel in retreat;
A Brother's blessing relights a pious flame.
The widow clings to faith's rebounding surge,
While accepting God's will, with grief in hand;
A bronze medallion is blessed to clear the dirge.
On rock of faith, with smiles, she takes her stand,
From deepest sorrow, follows heaven's urge,
Uplifted spirit, winged by soul's command.

DARWIN'S FAIRY TALE

Do acorns grow up to become thistles?
Does frightened rabbit shoot porcupine quills?
Do grains of wheat under heat sprout barley?
Has a Chimpanzee borne human baby?

Mendel's Law proved in vegetable Kingdom,
A like pattern in animal's total sum;
Laws of genetics, not found in attics,
Prove Darwin's theory wrong by mathematics.

The charts of hybrid litter expectancy
Are always exact mathematically;
Saturation of Mink's pigmentation changed
But specie form is never disarranged.

Have you seen a pansy face emerge
From the lovely hybrid tea rose splurge?
The rose rarely throws a sport coloration,
As peppermint stripes by white carnation.

God's patterns are set as the sun on high
Or the moon orbiting in starry sky –
Darwin said in late years he felt the urge
To retract the non-fact written in his book
But he lacked the courage to face the out-look.

BRIDGE OF LOVE

Yesterday I stood on the bridge of sighs,
Now I have grown much more wise.
I bow before Almighty God's will
At the fountain of His love drink my fill.
Singing of my Savior's love and beauty
There is new joy in doing my duty;
Spanning a wide abyss before my eyes;
A bridge of love and prayer to paradise.

ON THE STEEP ASCENT

See the Cross emblazoned on the dark sky.
Bright flame lights up pall-canopied day.
God's own love is an ever-burning flame,
our eternal heritage of pure delight,
therefore sing no threnody but happier song.

It is easier for God to reach down to men
than for man to reach up to Him again.
Let us keep in tune with His Great Spirit,
always keep a smile to light the way
for another pilgrim on the steep ascent.

GOD'S SECRETS

We plant the seed,
God decided what it will be.
Did you ever plant a "wait and see"
and find the answer in the bloom?
Designed before the upward thrust,
the pattern is His own,
stamped long before the seed is sown;
a grain of wheat, a whole field grows.

Before you grew,
the pattern was pure and sweet
when stamped upon your soul
as on the grain of wheat.

DREAMER'S GOLD

I hold the cast of truest joy
Within my own two priceless hands.
Reward is in my own employ.
I build not on shifting arid sands,
Lay corner stone with careful art,
Quoin from gold of dreams in my heart.

FOREVER-NOW

In the Forest of Forever-now
It first seems dark as night
A waking-dream-like state of fear
To face the shock unknown and near,
Before the spirit-eyes see light,
A change earth-school did not allow,
In forest of Forever-now.

In forest of Forever-now
A Christian spirit finds retreat;
Beloved voices from out the past
Come in the flooding dawn at last,
He tries to find the mercy seat
When he recalls the Savior's vow
In Forest of Forever-now.

In Forest of Forever-now
Reborn again in spirits youth
The Guardian-angel souls await
To lead them through the open gate,
Familiar voices chanting truth,
Assuming duties that endow
In Forest of Forever-now.

PAEAN OF JOY

On earth he knew only darkness of night
For all his life he groped in densest fog,
He never knew or saw this world aright
But leaned on Anna, see-ing eye trained dog.
Then Door of Light opened, released the soul,
The pall of darkness gone by divine plan;
In wondrous spirit life, God made him whole;
Once blind, now is a joyful, thankful man.
Since he has passed beyond the Great Divide,
The glad surprise is in his soul to stay,
To find clear sight is on the other side.
Forevermore he will know light of day!
With songs of praise for Heaven-glow so bright
He bends his knees before the Lord's great light.

TREE OF KNOWLEDGE

Living tree
of knowledge of good and evil
has many branches.
Upon this tree is engraved
history of the human race,
rise and fall of civilizations,
science and the arts;
prophecy, poetry, religions
of the world, ecology,
God's blue-print of space,
the firmament and the waters
that cradle the earth,
their myriad forms of life;
nuclear fission,
Pearl Harbor, Hiroshima, Nagasaki,
grim and terrible mission!
Knowledge of Good and Evil –
Herein is the future of Man.

INFINITE LOVE

Time is like the sifting sands
So rapidly slipping through
Our tightly closed hands
Time will never loiter
Memory always lingers
Divine giver of Life
Omnipresent Deity
And purest Love
The Our Father
All Glorious
In wisdom
Majestic
Love
Is Alpha
And Omega
Light - Life
Eternal Circle
Creator of all
Dominion and power
All good – Over-Soul
Substance of miracles
Divine Light and Wisdom
A point in ordered space
Where time and infinity meet
To merge in primordial essence

INVITATION TO A PARTY

September with its golden harvest morn,
dew fresh, sun-warmed, a day for a party.
The corn is ripe and ready for the feast,
in the old farm house where the first white
twins were born in Seattle, Washington.
The old fireplace with its wooden mantel,
its lovely wood sponged carefully with tea
polished as clean as could be.
Here in early days the twin girl babies
were placed in cigar boxes, lined with cotton;
pioneers had no hospital facilities.
Big logs were burning both night and day
to keep the temperature incubator-right.
Eye-dropper fed, tiny mouths hushed their cry.
In this spacious house many souls were born,
a few died.
Big families loved, laughed and cried.
This house breathed of love and hospitality.
It was the dinner-party's locality,
the outlook a railroad and Boeing Air Field.
The old orchard now forms a leafy shield
from the modern world's hub of the wheel.

In fun I was asked to read all their palms,
in the same spirit I responded.
Holding the hand of a handsome young man,
I saw him lying on his deathbed
with life hanging by a slender thread.
I concentrated and the answer came

"His life will pick up and go on again,
although the doctor says no hope for him".

Ahead of the M.D. in my presage,
I told his young wife Berta, the message.
"When the time comes in your precious lives
when Bernard's life hangs in the balance,
during the weary hours of suspense
hold on to this message with might,
know he will surely recover again."

Christmas Eve, about three months later
Bernard's parents were called to his bedside
to join the anxious wife.
The doctor said "He will not see Christmas Day".
All night Berta clung to God's blessed assurance,
bringing sustaining endurance;
truly there could be nothing in His way.
When Bernard survived pneumonia virus
this miracle served to inspire us.
What a divine privilege to be able to help
in times of great emotional stress.

GLASS HOUSES

In the Hollywood Green-houses glass broods over acres
of roses,
carnations; orchid plants reaching with tendril-fingered
hands,
clinging to wooden shelves. I am intrigued by their
fingers.
No other species has hands like human hands.
Suddenly a voice "Come out, hurry, hurry, a tornado!"
Outside: purple-black sky, a boa-constrictor dark funnel
whirls
toward the glass houses.
Standing in suspense, picturing awful destruction by
centrifugal
force, I pray "O God please make the tornado veer at a
right-angle
to head for Lake Washington to dissipate centrifugal
energy over
water where it can do no damage." . . . .
The twister veers, rises above the hill and spins to the
lake
with no damage done.
Mindless tornado forced to obey UNLIMITED MIND.
Prayer is the Aladdin's Lamp and God the Jinni of
Miracles.

MIRACLE OF MY HEART

The pounding heart, strangling pain was cutting off my
breath.
A police ambulance arrives with oxygen, takes me to
the hospital,
to intensive care.
I leave the hospital in time to attend the Poets State
convention
at Sacramento, where stabbing pain starts again at the
Senator Hotel.
My soul hears these words "My heart is one with the
Sacred Heart of Jesus".
I realize I am given a miracle formula to help me. I
repeat the formula.
It works! The pounding, the stabbing pain stops at
once. Miracle of
miracles! Thanks be to God. Thanks to Our Dear
Lord Jesus, the Son,
Master of Miracles, Savior and Eternal Friend.

IMMORTAL SOUL

God is not always invisible to me
For He is Reality.
The Divine spark of Life He placed within
Will remain His eternally;
Christ proved this Truth to be.
Faith in Him is empathy.
"I and my Father are One".
He will hold my hand when this long day is done,
I shall not fear to tread the path my Savior trod
Held by the Hand of God,
He will lead me through Death's unknown portal.
I know my soul is immortal!